Drew Carnwath

Two Plays

Johnnyville: An Official Secrets Act

Total Body Washout

Playwrights Canada Press
Toronto • Canada

Johnnyville: An Official Secrets Act and *Total Body Washout*

Playwrights Canada Press
54 Wolseley St., 2nd fl. Toronto, Ontario CANADA M5T 1A5
Tel: (416) 703-0201 Fax: (416) 703-0059
e-mail: orders@puc.ca http://www.puc.ca

Playwrights Canada Press acknowledges the support of The Canada Council for the Arts for our publishing programme and the Ontario Arts Council.

Cover photo: Diana Kolpak
Photo of Drew Carnwath: Helen Tansey

Canadian Cataloguing in Publication Data

Carnwath, Drew
Johnnyville: an official secrets act: and, Total body washout
Plays

ISBN 0-88754-555-6

I. Title. Title: Total body washout

PS8555.A7S54J63 1998. C812'.54 C98-930157-3
PR9199.3.C37J63 1998

First edition: May 1998. First Printing September 1999.
Printed and bound by Hignell Printing at Winnipeg, Manitoba, Canada.

Author's Notes

These plays would not have been possible, on page or on stage, without Diana Kolpak. From the first time I approached her with an early draft of *Total Body Washout*, to the last time we closed a show, her belief in the work has been a comfort and an inspiration. I will not forget Diana's encouragement, her twins Passion and Compassion, and her fast and furious red felt-tipped pen.

I also wish to thank the Alumnae Theatre in Toronto, where both plays had their first public performance at Alumnae's New Ideas Festival (1993 and 1994, respectively).

Thank you to Urjo Kareda and Andy McKim, and other writers in the 1996-97 Playwrights Unit at the Tarragon Theatre.

I am indebted to Bob White at Alberta Theatre Projects, who first commissioned *Johnnyville* for the 1993 playRITES Festival.

A special thanks to the cast and crew of each version of each of these plays — their hard work, their trust, and their input were a constant help to me.

Finally, and most important, I wish to thank my family. I love you all.

•••••••

Drew Carnwath is a playwright, actor, and musician who lives in Toronto. A member of Tarragon Theatre's 1996-97 Playwrights' Unit, Drew was also a member of The Advanced Actors' Company at The Banff Centre from 1993 to 1995. His plays have been produced in New York, Montreal, Kingston, Edmonton, and Vancouver; and his latest play, "I Dream of the Living", won First Prize in the 1996 Canadian National Playwrighting Competition (One-Act). Drew is currently a producer and writer at CTV Television in Toronto.

JOHNNYVILLE: AN OFFICIAL SECRETS ACT

dedicated to the two Gords
Lightfoot and Downie
two great Canadian storytellers

where do we go from here
the words are coming out all weird
where are you now when i need you

they brought in the CIA
the tanks and the whole marines
to blow me away to blow me sky high

Thom Yorke, "The Bends"

Production History

Johnnyville: An Official Secrets Act was originally commissioned by Bob White for the Alberta Theatre Projects PLAYrites Festival, 1994.

It was later expanded and produced in Toronto at The Alumnae Theatre New Ideas Festival in 1995, with the following cast and crew:

DOYLE	David Petrie
JOHNNY	Ross McKie
ALISA	Elyssa Livergant

Directed by Diana Kolpak
Designed by Wendy Akerboom

Johnnyville: An Official Secrets Act was later produced in Toronto by Whetstone Productions, under the title *Hide and Seek: Two Plays by Drew Carnwath.* The production credits were as above, except John Healy performed the role of DOYLE, and it was produced by Donna Gall.

Characters

DOYLE

ALISA

JOHNNY

Prologue

Music: Strains of a waltz by Strauss. Lights up to reveal JOHNNY *and* ALISA *dancing.*

DOYLE *enters and gives the dancing couple a cursory glance.* DOYLE *gently cuts in while* ALISA, *unaware, has her eyes closed.*

Music fades, but JOHNNY *continues to dance by himself, slowly, until he is almost off.* JOHNNY *motions to say something, exchanges a look with* DOYLE, *then stops himself. He dances off.*

DOYLE *dances* ALISA *over to a chair and gently sits her down.* ALISA *looks for* JOHNNY. JOHNNY *is gone.*

DOYLE *prepares a hypodermic needle for* ALISA. *He rolls up her sleeve; she offers no resistance.* DOYLE *motions to inject the needle.*

Then: the bright light of a camera flash. For a brief moment we see the following image superimposed: A black-and-white police photo of a murder victim, whose face is badly disfigured.

Blackout.

Scene One

Single light on JOHNNY. *He wears pajamas and a white terry bathrobe.*

JOHNNY There's this dream I have? Danny Kaye is teaching me how to dance. Danny Kaye. I have them a lot. What I call Famous Dead Celebrity dreams. And when I wake up, it's kind of a nice feeling: communicating with the afterlife and all.

Henry Fonda. Lucille Ball. Fatty Arbuckle — that was a good one. Mama Cass.

Actually that was an exception. That time I dreamt I was the guy who made Mama Cass the ham sandwich. You know — the sandwich. Well not many people know this, but it wasn't really the sandwich that killed her. In fact she took one bite of the sandwich, left it by her bed, and later had a heart attack in her sleep and died.

In the dream it was the day after she died and I was running around trying to tell people: "It wasn't my fault! I didn't kill Mama Cass! It wasn't even the sandwich that killed her!"

But no one would listen to me: "Oh you're the guy. I'm sure you must feel awful."

Where was I? Oh, yeah — Danny Kaye. The thing is, I usually know for sure if the Famous Dead Celebrity in question is really dead. Even while I'm dreaming it. But in the dream with Danny Kaye, he was so alive, so vivid. He wore a top hat and tails, and he smiled at me. And he was teaching me how to dance.

JOHNNY *dances. He's not very good.*

JOHNNY Then I wake up, it's still the middle of the night, and I — I'm so mad, because I can't remember if Danny Kaye is dead yet. In real life. Which shouldn't matter, I know, but it upsets me, and I have to find out. I reach for the phone, and —

Well who do you call at three a.m. to find out if a particular famous person is in fact still with us? There must be some kind of 24-hour service, right? Well of course the answer is no. There isn't.

I know this is trivial. I know there are more important things for a person such as myself to get hung up about. I accept that. But I had forgotten about my dream with Danny Kaye, and how I felt when I couldn't remember if he was dead, until this moment right now. And the thing is — I still don't know.

It ruined a perfectly good dream.

Scene Two

Single bright light on ALISA. *She is sitting in an interrogation room. The moment recalled.*

ALISA Okay, you win. I am willing to admit. There is such a thing as love. Even your kind of love.

Every summer from the time I was eleven until I was fifteen, my parents sent me to Ireland to live with my aunt in the country. On that last summer, the fifteen-year-old summer, I met my first boyfriend. Larry Lugg.

For the longest time I thought the "Lugg" part was just a joke, a nickname his friends had given him. I mean, you know. He was kind of big. But that was his name. Larry Lugg. Larrylugg.

He wore a big woolen sweater, olive green, and he had one thick eyebrow that went clear across his forehead, and he smelled of talcum powder and gasoline. I never spoke to him. I never spoke to anyone. I was kind of terrified of the world. I think he liked that in me.

He was the first person who ever kissed me, too. I mean really kissed me, not like the chocolatey kisses you get from weird old distant relatives every Christmas. Kiss kiss.

I was in a tree. And so was Larry. He was older than me, he was at least... seventeen. Anyway, there we are, me and Larry Lugg, not saying a word to each other up in that tree, and suddenly he reaches out to put his hand behind my neck. I remember it was one hand, because if he'd used both hands he would have fallen. Out of the tree.

So he reaches out to me, only... I think he's trying to flick a bug off my face, and so I yell: "What? What is it? Get it off me!"

Well. He kissed me. And it was wonderful, and warm, and a little bit wet the way those kisses are supposed to be. And then somehow he put both his arms around me. And to this day I can't figure out how Larry Lugg kept from falling to a tragic death by kissing me, a virgin, up in a tree, with no hands. Something had to be supporting him up there.

Maybe it was me.

I was so scared after that, I just wanted to die. I went and lay down in the middle of the road. I wanted to get run over. I was so filled with stuff I'd never felt before, that I knew I had to die. But of course there are no cars in the Irish countryside. Everybody walks.

So I lay there in the road for what must have been hours. And after a while the feeling went away. I stopped feeling romantic and I stopped feeling scared and I looked around and it was getting dark and pretty soon the only thing I was feeling was cold. So I got up and went home.

And nothing since. Nothing pure, anyway. Things get so complicated. I lost my virginity... in stages. We need to qualify everything. Why is that? Why are we so compelled to label the Really Big Emotions? This is romance, that is lust. This is my friend, that is my love slave. Ridiculous? Maybe.

But for me? If I don't know exactly who and what I'm dealing with I'm going to fall between the cracks of what's left unsaid. So: Seems I was right after all, and you were wrong. Is that what you wanted to hear?

Scene Three

Very loud industrial dance music. Pulsating lights: a dance club. ALISA *is standing alone at the bar, holding a half-full bottle of beer, swaying to the music.*

Then, more lights reveal JOHNNY. *They are not "together," but somehow they've managed to end up standing beside one another. They shout the first half of the scene, to rise above the music.*

ALISA Hi!

JOHNNY What?!

ALISA Hello!

JOHNNY Oh! I thought you said "Hi."

ALISA I did!

JOHNNY What? *(beat)* I'm Johnny!

ALISA WHAT?

JOHNNY MY... NAME... IS... JOHNNY!

ALISA Really? I thought it was Abba! *(beat)* You know, "Dancing Queen?" *(beat)* "See that girl, watch that scene..."?

JOHNNY What's your name?!

ALISA Ukraine?! I think they're Swedish! *(beat)* I'm Irish!

JOHNNY Hullo, Iris!

ALISA On my mother's side. My father's Dutch!

JOHNNY I'm Johnny!

ALISA I know, I hate these places too! *(beat, explaining)* I'm here with friends!

ALISA *looks around, and shrugs.*

ALISA I must have lost them!

Uncomfortable pause. They both pretend to look around the bar, shrug, and then they begin to move a little to the music. JOHNNY *is still a bad dancer.* ALISA *is remarkably good.*

The music changes to a ballad. DOYLE *enters the bar. He is not drinking.* JOHNNY *and* ALISA *look around the bar again, then catch each other's eye.* ALISA *forces a laugh.*

ALISA So! I — do I know you from somewhere?

JOHNNY Ummm....

ALISA *smacks her head with her palm.*

ALISA Oh, what a cornball thing to say, I'm sorry —

JOHNNY No, I'm sorry — you don't know me —

ALISA So am I. I mean —

JOHNNY No, what I mean is — *(beat)* Are you always this tall?

ALISA *looks at him in disbelief.*

JOHNNY You might be mistaking me for —

ALISA Someone shorter?

JOHNNY I can't see your feet! You could be wearing heels!

ALISA *lifts one leg way up, showing* JOHNNY *her shoe.*

JOHNNY Oh, I see. That's, uh —

ALISA Flats!

JOHNNY Right! Yes. Flat as a board. Heh heh.

Beat. ALISA *sits, and invites* JOHNNY *to do the same.*

ALISA Are you here with friends?

JOHNNY No.

ALISA Do you come here — *(stopping herself)* Have you been here before?

JOHNNY No.

ALISA Ah.

JOHNNY I'm looking for someone —

Light change. Straight to interrogation scene.

Scene Four

DOYLE *and* ALISA. ALISA *is seated in the chair, as in Scene One.*

DOYLE I'm looking for someone

DOYLE *produces a photograph. Brief tableau, as the image from the photo is superimposed over the scene: A black-and-white mug shot of* JOHNNY. DOYLE *hands photo to* ALISA. *She glances at the photo, then looks away, unmoved.*

DOYLE Do you recognize him?
Do you know him?
Look closely. Have you met him before?
Have you seen him... anywhere?
On the street, at work, in a restaurant?
In a bar? *(beat)*
Look again, into his eyes, that helps.
Look in his eyes.

ALISA *gives another cursory look.*

DOYLE He's gone missing. For two weeks now. And we're anxious to have a chat with him. We believe you may be able to help us locate him. Look again. Please. Sometimes it takes a while.

ALISA *doesn't respond.* DOYLE *hands her another photograph. A black-and-white image of* ALISA *and* JOHNNY *dancing is superimposed over the scene.*

DOYLE: You and the suspect were seen together on the night of September the twelfth, at an establishment called The Hop and Grape. Known locally as The Hope and Grope. Curious. You don't know the guy.

ALISA I have seen him before. He's just a guy I met at a bar.

DOYLE So what happened?

ALISA Nothing. We had a drink. We danced. We talked. I went home. Alone.

DOYLE What did you talk about?

ALISA I don't know. *(*JOHNNY*'s voice joins her's)* "Philosophy, art, nihilism, whatever."

DOYLE Did he try to pick you up? Did you come to the bar alone, or with friends? Please. Answer the question.

ALISA I was alone.

DOYLE And where is he now?

ALISA I don't know.

DOYLE You haven't seen the suspect since then?

ALISA No.

DOYLE He didn't, say, give you a phone number, an address, anywhere he could be reached?

ALISA No.

DOYLE I see. So. On the night of September the twelfth you went to The Hop and Grape, alone. You met up with the suspect, had one drink, danced, talked about philosophy-art-nihilism-whatever; after which he tried, unsuccessfully, to pick you up, and then you went home. Alone. That it?

ALISA No. I also slept.

DOYLE *pulls up a chair.*

DOYLE Alright. Now how about telling me what really happened.

DOYLE *spins her chair around to face him. Fiercely:*

I don't want to make this difficult. For either of us. So either you can tell me everything you know, and you're free to go. Or you can sit here and continue to play dumb. It's up to you. But you're not leaving until I'm satisfied I've got the truth.

ALISA Who are you, anyway?

DOYLE I work for the government.

ALISA Whose?

DOYLE I'm sorry?

ALISA No, you're not sorry. You just didn't hear the question. Whose government do you work for?

DOYLE Ours. Mine and yours. Of course. I don't think you understand the severity of this case — or the danger you've put yourself in. The suspect is an extremely dangerous individual. He's wanted for several heinous crimes. Treason, espionage, murder —

ALISA Johnny's a spy?

DOYLE I'm sor — what did you call him?

ALISA Johnny. He told me his name was Johnny.

DOYLE *(making a note)* Slippery fellow. Johnny Doe — that's good. You see he changes his identity faster than most people change their mind —

ALISA You've got the wrong guy. The guy I met isn't capable of the stuff you're talking about. Espionage? Please. He got lost looking for the washrooms.

DOYLE *makes a note of this.*

ALISA Oh, come on.

DOYLE Don't underestimate the skill and ease with which he can appear to be someone he's not.

ALISA Do you always talk like that?

DOYLE Like what?

ALISA Forget it.

DOYLE I take my work very seriously. I suggest you do the same. For two years now, a team of well-trained and highly efficient agents has been tracking down the suspect —

ALISA Johnny —

DOYLE And all of a sudden he's spotted at a busy downtown bar. Why?

ALISA Thirsty?

DOYLE Don't — ! No. Your "Johnny" doesn't drink. After two years of eluding us at each step, "Johnny" risks everything by going public. And who is he seen with? You. He chose you. Why? You must have something, some information he desperately wants to get his hands on. What do you suppose that is?

ALISA Let's get a couple of things straight. Johnny didn't "choose" me — just maybe I chose him. And it wasn't information he was trying to get his hands on, believe me. In any case my personal life is none of your business —

DOYLE My business involves a highly dangerous man who is wanted for several crimes against the state —

ALISA Whose state?

DOYLE Ours! Mine and yours, of course! Are you through? You're not nearly as amusing to me as you find yourself —

ALISA What does any of this have to do with —

DOYLE Where is Johnny?

ALISA I don't know! I'm telling you — Look, you say the man you're looking for doesn't drink? Well, Johnny sure tossed them back, faster than I could make —

Beat.

DOYLE You were saying? You took him home. Didn't you?

ALISA Maybe. Maybe I did, maybe — what difference does it make?

DOYLE What was it — a fling? One-night stand?

ALISA More or less.

DOYLE Well?

ALISA Less. Definitely less.

Scene Five

JOHNNY *swoops down and picks up* ALISA, *carrying her piggyback into* ALISA*'s apartment. Laughter.*

JOHNNY Nice place.

ALISA You like?

JOHNNY "Ya. I like. Is good." All this on a programmer's salary? What is it you do, exactly?

ALISA You know, stuff. Drink?

JOHNNY Whatever you're having.

ALISA Okey dokey, smokey.

ALISA *exits.* JOHNNY *begins to poke around the apartment, looking at books and papers.*

JOHNNY He-ey —

ALISA *(off)* What?

JOHNNY That sure is one wizened apple ya got there —

ALISA It's not an apple, goomba!

JOHNNY Oh. It's not? Oh.

ALISA It's an avocado pit!

JOHNNY I knew that. I just wanted to use the word "wizened."

ALISA You put it in a jar, give it plenty of water and sunlight, and then you wait for it to grow....

JOHNNY Like Sea Monkeys?

ALISA What?

JOHNNY Nothing.

ALISA *returns with two multi-coloured tropical drinks with much fruit garnish and umbrellas. She hands one to* JOHNNY. *He eyes it suspiciously.*

JOHNNY By the way, I think I should tell you: Johnny isn't my real name.

ALISA Really.

JOHNNY Yes. Really, it's —

ALISA Call-me-Ishmael?

JOHNNY Goomba. I'm kind of sensitive about it.

ALISA I'll be careful.

JOHNNY "You'll be dead!!" *(beat)* That's, um, a line from my favourite movie.

ALISA *(beat)* Right. Well. Cheers!

JOHNNY Prozit!

JOHNNY *drains the entire drink in one gulp.*

JOHNNY Mmmm, very nice. Skol. From Vladivostok. Not available in Canada. Pity.

ALISA *(casually)* Present from a friend. You can taste the difference between —

JOHNNY It's certainly not from Ireland.

ALISA How did you know I was — You *did* hear me in the bar! "Hullo, Iris!" As if!

JOHNNY Hear what? Your friend has good taste.

Beat. ALISA *takes his glass, and exits to refill it.*

ALISA *(off)* I don't, um, normally go to singles bars!

JOHNNY Me neither!

ALISA It's just that — well, my friends and I, we —

JOHNNY I hope —

ALISA Yes?

JOHNNY I feel bad, about —

ALISA What?

ALISA *returns with another drink for* JOHNNY.

JOHNNY Your friends. I hope they weren't too upset that you —

ALISA Ditched them? Not at all. Besides, my friends are harmless. Like you.

JOHNNY Like me?

ALISA I mean that in a good way.

JOHNNY Of course.

ALISA I'm very good at reading people, if you want to know the truth.

JOHNNY *points to himself.*

ALISA Oh, like a book. I prefer to surround myself with unthreatening people. Makes life less complicated.

JOHNNY I'm uncomplicated?

ALISA You? You're a cinch. You're just like any other guy, only more so. *(beat)* Except for one thing: I can't figure out if you want to sleep with me. Or not.

JOHNNY *swallows; pretends he didn't.*

ALISA I mean, most guys, you can tell right away.

JOHNNY Oh, yeah. *(beat)* How?

ALISA I can tell a guy wants to sleep with me if tries to be really interesting about —

DOYLE*'s voice joins* ALISA*'s:*

ALISA "Philosophy, art, nihilism, whatever." Anything but sex. It's amazing the things we pretend to be fascinated by, just to get in bed. Nobody talks anymore. I mean, really talks. It's all intellectual foreplay.

JOHNNY *plays with the umbrella in his empty glass.*

ALISA So, okay, so I see a guy, maybe I meet him for the first time. And all of a sudden he's The One. Mister Right-You-Are. It's crazy! I haven't said a word to him, but in the space of about seven seconds I want to spend the rest of my life with this man.

JOHNNY So what happens?

ALISA He opens his mouth —

Beat.

JOHNNY Oh —

ALISA And proceeds to talk about a recent Cezanne exhibit, Social Darwinism, his lame theories on the latest serial killer, boy-o-boy how 'bout that Berlin Wall? Well, Studmuffin, I have a television set too, you know. Everything's been said. There's nothing left to *not* talk about anymore.

JOHNNY Except sex.

ALISA Exactly. Which is why I can't figure you out.

JOHNNY What about your friend? Mr. Skol.

ALISA Oh, no. Just friends. He's much older.

JOHNNY Ah. *(beat)* I don't mind talking about it.

ALISA What?

JOHNNY It. You know.

ALISA Sex.

JOHNNY Yeah.

ALISA Great!

Three full beats.

JOHNNY You start.

ALISA *begins to undo* JOHNNY*'s shirt.*

ALISA Okay. What do you like? What do you... enjoy?

JOHNNY I — well, I enjoy — you know, sex —

ALISA What'd I tell you? Harmless.

JOHNNY I'm not harmless.

ALISA You are! What's the worse thing you've ever done? Ever.

JOHNNY I'd rather talk about sex —

She continues to undress him.

ALISA Answer the question.

JOHNNY Let's see. The worst thing, the worst thing — Well, this one time, when I was in grade three, I —

ALISA Time's up! Answer the question!

Light change. Interrogation scene.

Scene Six

DOYLE and ALISA.

DOYLE Answer the question!

ALISA *(still in previous scene, confused)* What —

DOYLE Where is Johnny?

ALISA I don't know.

DOYLE *(deep sigh, produces a file)* According to our records you've been associated with the terrorist CLF since 1980 —

ALISA I broke off all of those ties! I've had nothing to do with The Front since... a long time ago.

DOYLE Why is that?

ALISA I woke up. I realized that politics — polemics — weren't going to change the world. Even radical terrorist politics. Besides, I'm sure you know how things at the CLF got... out of control. Everyone running around with a vague sense of panic and paranoia — smear campaigns, corruption, disinformation... fear. People were afraid they were being watched, which they probably were. It got to the point where I stopped knowing who the real enemy was.

DOYLE I can tell you —

ALISA Yes, I know: Your bosses on the Capital. But after a while... who can you trust?

DOYLE Indeed. Who can you trust.

ALISA I've learned it's better — best — not to trust anyone.

DOYLE That's a lonely existence.

ALISA You don't know anything about me.

DOYLE Perhaps not. Don't you trust me? *(*ALISA *laughs)* You trusted Johnny enough to take him home, didn't you ?

ALISA *motions to retaliate, then stops herself. Controlled.*

DOYLE Never mind, we'll get to that. Corruption in the CLF And you had no part of it?

ALISA No. Honestly? I wasn't strong enough to resist corruption. That's why I left.

DOYLE But you were strong enough to fight for a piece of it, weren't you?

ALISA I don't know what you mean.

DOYLE Don't you? *(beat)* So. You "broke all ties with the CLF." What year was that?

ALISA Over a period of several years. Although my involvement was just peripheral, it's not like the CLF is some dinner party you can just excuse yourself from.

DOYLE You were pressured to stay.

ALISA Of course. The lack of trust goes both ways. Everyone was so busy keeping tabs on everyone else's activities, falling over each other, walking backwards trying not to be noticed. Keeping secrets became... an obsession. Even official secrets.

Lights up on JOHNNY.

Scene Seven

Interlude. Tableau on the previous scene. JOHNNY *speaks to the audience. Matter of fact:*

JOHNNY Under the Official Secrets Act
it is a criminal offence to disclose documents
leak information
or otherwise communicate any files
classified as confidential.

Any person or persons under suspicion
of breaking the Official Secrets Act
known as a whistle blower
is considered a serious threat
to National Security.

Such a person can and will be charged
tried
convicted
and sentenced in absolute secrecy.

No media coverage.
No appeals.
No re-trial.
No joke.

Official. Secrets. Act.
I like the sound of that.
What makes an act "secret"?
What makes a secret "official"?
And just how will I know when I am secure —
nationally speaking?

Scene Eight

ALISA *joins* JOHNNY *in bed. The morning after.*

ALISA Tumescence.

JOHNNY Tongue.

ALISA Teeming.

JOHNNY That's a good one.

ALISA You see? Words that begin with "T" are the sexiest.

JOHNNY What about romantic words? Anyone can have sex. I mean, anyone is capable of having sex. Romance is much harder. *(beat)* Paraffin.

ALISA Prolong.

JOHNNY Priapism. Sorry.

ALISA Persuasion.

JOHNNY Good. *(beat)* Panacea.

ALISA Panacea?

JOHNNY It means a healing remedy, a tonic —

ALISA I know what it means!

JOHNNY Really? I had to look it up. *(beat)* Murmur.

ALISA Mmmm. Murmur. I like that one.

JOHNNY It's one of the three easiest-to-pronounce words in the English language. Mur-mur.

ALISA Really. What are the three most difficult words to say?

JOHNNY I can think of three.

Beat. She ignores this.

ALISA Words that begin with 'K.' Um... Kismet.

JOHNNY *gives her a long, slow, wet kiss.*

JOHNNY Ooops. Did you say "kiss me?"

They embrace, ravenously, and begin to disrobe.

JOHNNY Youch!

ALISA What?

JOHNNY I think I sprained my — my —

ALISA What? Sprained your what?

JOHNNY I'm not sure yet —

Phone rings. Beat. They eye one another.

ALISA I should probably — I should, you know, get —

JOHNNY *(laughing)* Go, go!

ALISA *goes to the phone. Lights up on* DOYLE, *also on the phone.*

ALISA Hello?

DOYLE It's me.

ALISA Hello?

DOYLE Yes. I know.

ALISA Hello? Anybody there?

DOYLE We're in the thick of —

ALISA They hung up.

DOYLE I'll do the best I can —

JOHNNY Who was it?

DOYLE I promise.

ALISA Wrong number.

DOYLE I promise.

Lights down on JOHNNY. *Interrogation room.* DOYLE *is still on the phone.*

Scene Nine

DOYLE *and* ALISA. DOYLE *on the phone.*

DOYLE Listen, I can't talk right now. Tell them I'll see them — I'll see them when I see them.

DOYLE *hangs up, and immediately goes back to his line of questioning.*

DOYLE During that time you had a long-standing liaison with the Minister of Defence. According to the *Toronto Chronicle*, you were a paid informant —

ALISA A mole. *(beat)* You can use the word. They called me a mole. My case was thrown out of court before we even went to trial. Look if you intend to drag that up, let me save you some time: I was innocent then and I'm innocent now. I'm sure it's all there in your magic files, anyway. Look it up.

DOYLE After your case was rejected, we noticed that a certain file went missing from the Minister's office. Perhaps you've heard of it? "The McGuffin Papers."

ALISA I've never heard of that file before. What's in it?

DOYLE That's confidential.

ALISA You want me to co-operate? Fine. You give me a straight answer, I'll give you one. You haul me out of my office like I'm the criminal, you make allegations you can't even support, you dredge up a part of my life that I kissed good-bye a long time ago.... How can I respond to information that you say is confidential? *(beat)* You're desperate. Aren't you? What will it take?

DOYLE Where. Is. Johnny?

ALISA I'd like to know that myself.

DOYLE You expect me to believe that? That someone you have been intimate with just up and disappears? Don't you find that a little odd?

ALISA Odd? Welcome to my life. I meet a guy, we actually have a few things in common, we're getting along great, I'm thinking, hey, this could really work, and then — BOOM! Before we even get, as you say, "intimate," he gets the Fear and hightails it out of there —

DOYLE Before you get intimate?

ALISA I can't possibly expect you to understand this, but sometimes it's enough to just talk.

DOYLE I see. So what did you and Johnny talk about?

Scene Ten

JOHNNY *alone.*

JOHNNY The sound of wind moving through the tall grass. The smell of sulphur from the hot springs.

ALISA *(joining him)* What else?

JOHNNY The colours were richer. The emerald green of a lake named Louise. Everything was so clearly defined, too. Like the thick black outlines of a colouring book. Long, drawn-out afternoons without detail and without punctuation.

All of the other families staying at the Jasper Park Lodge. And this figure, moving in front of me. She was —

We stayed in a cabin by the lake. At night the moms and dads went out dancing, and the babysitters ran up and down the boardwalk, checking on the kids. I was so bored, I wanted to make something, I don't know, like hand puppets. So I cut the material from the curtains, this great tartan. And after slicing enough for two puppets, at least, I needed some help to make the heads. So I called out to the sitter. No response.

I went to the window, and looked out to see her locked arm-in-arm with a boyfriend, these two dark muted figures against the lake. They were kissing in a way that my mom and dad never kissed. When she came in, I could feel her warmth.

She picked me up, quietly scolded me, and put me to bed. And I decided to fall in love with her. I couldn't have been more than five years old.

Looking back, I know I couldn't possibly have been alone. But on that night she crashed into my holiday of ice-cream parlours, penny arcades, and swimming lessons. I had no idea who she was, or even what she was, but — she was there, you see, and my mother was out dancing.

ALISA First love.

JOHNNY First and last.

She removes a ring from around her neck, and gives it to JOHNNY.

JOHNNY Hey, what —

ALISA I want you to wear it.

He puts it on.

ALISA Tell me more.

JOHNNY Nothing to tell.

ALISA Oh, come on.

JOHNNY I thought you could read me... like a book, isn't that what you said?

ALISA Yeah, so maybe I'm wrong. It does happen from time to time.

JOHNNY What about you?

ALISA I'm an open book, too.

JOHNNY Oh yeah? So how do I know I'm seeing the real you?

ALISA The real me? You sound like a self-help book. Besides, there's no such thing as the real anyone. We all just present versions. Doncha think? *(beat)* Johnny?

JOHNNY Kiss me.

ALISA Kismet.

They kiss. A tableau. DOYLE *enters and looks on with detachment.*

DOYLE Love. From what I can tell, love is sloppy, love — clouds the mind and weakens the constitution. And unlike its evil twin hate, love can be used up. Pace yourself. Save your energy for the real enemy.

JOHNNY *exits.* ALISA *is still frozen in tableau. Then: interrogation scene.*

Scene Eleven

DOYLE *and* ALISA.

DOYLE Pssst! Hey —

ALISA *"wakes" and crosses back to the chair.*

ALISA I felt sorry for him.

DOYLE Go on.

ALISA He'd been out of work —

DOYLE Out of work? And what did Johnny do for a living? What did he say he "worked" at?

ALISA *(quietly)* He didn't say, exactly. I assumed he was between jobs —

DOYLE Cry me a freakin' river.

ALISA *(rising)* You don't know what you're talking about. Johnny is no criminal. He didn't want anything from me but a little attention and affection. And I gave it, willingly. We all want that. Even you. Someone as beautiful and anonymous as the people who lay us down in our dreams. Tell me: When was the last you felt that?

DOYLE Sit down. Now, I'm going to strike a deal with you. You tell me where Johnny is, and you're free to go. No further questions.

ALISA I don't know where he is.

DOYLE You want to protect him. I understand that. But I can assure you, the last thing we want to do is to harm the man.

ALISA I. Don't. Know.

DOYLE *(sighing)* Certain tenets of The McGuffin File were descrambled by our intercept antennae, transmissions that we sourced at CLF headquarters on Heron Road; and since —

ALISA What makes you think I had access to that, or any other information? Simply being a member of an organization doesn't guarantee I have the slightest clue of what's going on. I'm sure you understand that. Secret Circus.

DOYLE Tell me about your liaison with the Minister of Defence. *(beat)* Some say that "liaison" extended well beyond Party protocol.

ALISA Some say that?

DOYLE *(holding up a file)* Some say.

ALISA I don't belong to any Party anymore. I don't "belong" to anyone.

DOYLE *(moving in)* Not even to Johnny?

ALISA *motions to strike* DOYLE. DOYLE *grabs her arm and laughs. Cross-fade to* JOHNNY.

Scene Twelve

JOHNNY *alone.*

JOHNNY I am always inventing and re-inventing myself. Sometimes in dreams. But mostly in real life. And I am tired. I want to go away. I just want to go to a place where no one knows me, and start all over again. Just me. Haven't you ever wanted that? No past. Not even a future. Just a constantly changing ever-present. That's why I like motel rooms.

ALISA *enters.*

JOHNNY Haven't you ever wanted that?

ALISA No.

JOHNNY I don't believe you.

ALISA I mean, sure, I've always wanted to take that trip around the world, but —

BOTH "It would take so long to get back."

JOHNNY Hey. You're not supposed to know the punch line to my lame jokes.

ALISA Really. What am I supposed to know? Just how much am I allowed to know?

JOHNNY What do you mean?

ALISA Nothing.

JOHNNY Oh.

ALISA What were we talking about?

JOHNNY Um, re-inventing oneself. As in, have you ever wanted to —

ALISA The last time I re-invented myself? I got my colours done. I dressed like a "winter." I was so proud. Imagine my horror when I found out that, after all that, I was actually a "summer." *(mocking)* Oh, the shame. Couldn't show my face for weeks.

JOHNNY Is that, like, some kind of joke?

ALISA No.

JOHNNY You're making fun of me.

ALISA No. I love you.

JOHNNY Oh. You do? Oh. *(beat)* I don't know if I can, I mean —

ALISA I can't expect you to — I don't get it. You only let me get so close, and then you just — shut off.

JOHNNY Shut off —

ALISA You never talk about... anything! Not your work, not your friends, not your family. I mean, I'm all for privacy, but — I feel like a secret.

JOHNNY Secret? No, no —

ALISA I know, I shouldn't get mad —

JOHNNY Well, maybe instead of getting mad you should —

ALISA Get even?

JOHNNY Get even? What —

ALISA Get even madder —

JOHNNY No, no — What were we talking about?

ALISA Ummm.... re-inventing yourself. Motel rooms.

JOHNNY I'm talking about something else. Starting over.

ALISA I thought that's what we were doing. Together.

JOHNNY It is, but — I'm talking about — what happens to people, when they get involved. They lose something of themselves —

ALISA They? You mean you, don't you?

Beat.

JOHNNY I can't be with you, this way, I have to —

ALISA What is it? Tell me. I can handle the truth.

JOHNNY I'm not sure you can.

ALISA Oh, give me a little credit.

JOHNNY It's like I said, about being something I'm not —

ALISA Johnny. I just told you I loved you.

JOHNNY Yes. You did.

ALISA I can't expect you to feel the same way, but — Do you want to be with me?

JOHNNY Yes.

He embraces her. She closes her eyes, drifting off.

ALISA I don't understand you sometimes....

JOHNNY I know.

ALISA I'm so... tired....

JOHNNY *and* ALISA *fall asleep. Three full beats.*

JOHNNY *dreams:* DOYLE *enters, wearing a trenchcoat and fedora.*

JOHNNY Holy shit!

DOYLE Hello.

JOHNNY Orson Welles?

DOYLE Harry Lime, actually.

JOHNNY "The Third Man." What —

DOYLE *(as Orson Welles/Harry Lime)* "In Italy, for thirty years under the Borgias, they had warfare, terror, murder, and bloodshed — but they produced Michelangelo, Leonardo Da Vinci, and the Renaissance. In Switzerland, they had brotherly love, they had five-hundred years of democracy and peace — and what did they produce? The Cuckoo Clock. Remember who the real enemy is."

JOHNNY *rises from the bed and makes a quiet exit.* DOYLE *removes the trenchcoat and fedora. He holds the ring.*

DOYLE The plates are shifting. I can feel it.
And I intend to remain, untouched
here on *terra firma.*
And I will watch when the shit really flies
when there is nothing left but
the sound of teeth ripping through fur and flesh
the sight of cracked bones and severed entrails
the smell of burning hair and nails.

The world as we think we know it is collapsing.
Defence systems are breaking down.
Lies are rising to the surface.
The ideas we once held as truth are shifting
like plates under the earth.
And really, there is nothing we can do to prevent
what will no doubt be our inevitable, pathetic
demise. We cannot prepare for it.
We wait.

Two groups of people will emerge.
The first group will panic.
And panic will be on their faces
as they wait in the check-out lines
as they wait for a raise
as they wait in the pews
"Give me a sign!"

But the lies continue
as they make their pledges
go through the motions
lie about lying
and cling to whatever they can.
Usually, each other.

The second group will not panic
because they have no clue as to the inevitable.
They smile their ignorant smiles
and make their little transgressions
fill their time with fornications
and fables of Life On Earth.
A day at the circus.
Three ring circus.
They truly believe in the big lie.

And I will watch when
these two groups of people fall
through the cracks of their own beliefs
because I believe in order and discipline
and hard work.
Because. I believe in work.

Scene Thirteen

ALISA *wakes. She is alone.*

ALISA This morning I woke up early
I wasn't tired
I watched you sleep
for hours, it must have been
you were flat on your back
you didn't move.

But the funniest thing
all of a sudden you started to roll around
and say things I couldn't understand
you rocked back and forth like a child
just like a —

Your breathing went all crazy and uneven
you were fighting for purer air
like a sickness
but I didn't wake you up
I just watched
I just watched.

I reached out and put my hand on your forehead
something my parents used to do whenever I was sick.
It felt familiar to me.
It felt like home.

Well. It worked. You stopped rolling around.
Whatever it was, went away.
And I went back to sleep.

I was going to tell you about it, later
but when I woke up
you were no longer beside me.
Where did you go?
I don't belong to anyone, anymore.

Scene Fourteen

DOYLE *enters.*

DOYLE Not even to Johnny?

She rises to strike DOYLE *as before.* DOYLE *grabs her arm and laughs.*

DOYLE You fell in love with Johnny, didn't you?

ALISA Love is a myth. It's a big lie. Live free from the lies, I say, or die. And steer clear of entangling alliances.

DOYLE And the Minister of Defence?

ALISA A friend. Friendship is a lot more lasting than love —

DOYLE But not nearly as entertaining.

ALISA Look: As friends, the men in my life remain forever. As lovers, they're distractions. Sure, they enter my life innocently enough. Smiling. Doting. But pretty soon they creep under my fingernails, and slowly start to press up. They demand that I be someone else. Their ex-wife; their ex-lover. Their mother. "I'm just looking for companionship," they say. "Get a dog," I say.

DOYLE You're so tough.

ALISA You think so?

DOYLE No. You think you're hard-boiled, but you're not. You're about thirty seconds —

ALISA Did you make that up yourself?

DOYLE You know what I think? I think you fell in love. Johnny had you so duped, you fell madly in love with him. Tell me I'm wrong.

ALISA You're wrong.

DOYLE You're no sucker. But he had you in so deep, I'll bet that when you looked into his eyes he took you to another place. Didn't he? Johnnyville. The place we all want to go. You knew he didn't love you in return. But you wanted to believe in that special place so badly, you were willing to forgive that; forgive everything. Even when he left you. My mother always said: "If you look deep enough in someone's eyes, you can always find a bit of good." Even a lying scum like Johnny.

ALISA That's the second mistake your mother made —

DOYLE You don't even —

ALISA Look, the Johnny I know —

DOYLE The Johnny you know doesn't exist! He's a creation, a non-person who became exactly what you wanted him to be! That's his job!

ALISA You can't know what it was like.

DOYLE What was it like? Tell me, I'm curious. What does it feel like to give yourself over to someone so completely? Someone you hardly even know! You said you weren't the trusting type. You don't strike me as the kind of person who believes in love at first sight.

ALISA Why not? It saves a lot of time. *(beat)* I wasn't aware that I "struck" you at all.

DOYLE Oh, yes.

ALISA So, you're an expert on the subject —

DOYLE Love is a song on the radio. Love is an editorial. It's just an idea that occurs to other people, and it doesn't last. I see it everywhere I go, people giving up so much of themselves, making them weak. I can't stand that weakness, and the ignorance: In betraying what they love, they betray what's truest about themselves.

ALISA You poor, poor man. Look at you work so hard. It's an interesting theory. Too bad you don't believe a word of it yourself.

DOYLE You don't know me.

ALISA You haven't given me a chance —

DOYLE Alright. I want you to prove it to me. Really. Prove to me that what you and Johnny had was real.

ALISA What do want me to say? Make a show of it? Tell you that he brought me roses?

DOYLE *(genuine)* Did he?

ALISA Yes. Yes, he did, but —

DOYLE A real romantic.

ALISA In his own way, sure. I respect that.

DOYLE Roses don't show respect. They show intention.

ALISA Oh, for — I can see where this is going —

DOYLE What about sex?

ALISA What about it?

DOYLE Did he look you in the eye when he made love to you? Did he? And when you told him that you loved him, did you believe it when he said the words? Or maybe he never even said the words —

ALISA I know what you're trying to do. And it won't work. I guess some people are incapable of loving.

She touches DOYLE *on the cheek.*

ALISA Or being loved.

DOYLE *(pushing her hand away)* You no longer amuse me. In fact you bore me. All night long you've done nothing but sit there talking yourself in and out of one helluva spiderweb of lies. I'm tired of playing guessing games.

He hands her the ring from Scene Ten.

DOYLE *(matter of fact)* His body turned up yesterday by the river bank. Just five minutes from your apartment.

DOYLE *hands her a photo. The black-and-white police photo of a disfigured murder victim is superimposed on the scene, as in Scene One.*

DOYLE What a waste. We were so close. But evidently someone got to him before we did. I was afraid of that. Shame: All we wanted to do was offer him a job.

ALISA *(tears)* What?

DOYLE In our line of work, when an individual begins to make a lot of noise, he becomes a real threat. And that makes us very nervous. You know that. But you never, ever try to shut him down. It never works. No, you do the only sensible thing: Hire him. Better to have him working for us, than working for them. If the price is right.

DOYLE *takes out a handkerchief.*

DOYLE Here. If it's any comfort to you, he was killed en route to your apartment. So. Either you've been lying to me all along, and he was making a second attempt to get the file, or —

DOYLE *lifts her chin up.*

DOYLE He really liked you. Any thoughts?

She spits at him.

Either way. He was killed by your own people. Your friends at the CLF were on to him before we were. Whatever is in that file, The Front made damn sure Johnny didn't get to it. Oh, I know your involvement with The Front is anything but "peripheral." But like you said: Who can you trust?

ALISA You asshole.

DOYLE Here. This will make you feel better.

DOYLE *prepares hypodermic needle, as in the Prologue. She stares straight ahead, offering no resistance.*

DOYLE I know you know where that file is. Just tell me where, and you are free to walk out that door. But the more time we waste, the more likely the file will end up in the wrong hands. In fact I'll bet your apartment is being turned upside down right now by members of the CLF Perhaps even the very people who killed your boyfriend. *(beat)* Now: Are you willing to co-operate?

ALISA *nods a slow, steady "yes."* DOYLE *begins to inject the needle. Cross-fade.*

Scene Fifteen

JOHNNY *alone.*

JOHNNY People ask about the fear
that what I do for a living
brings me closer to death every day
it is a daily thing.

People ask about the rush
and the rush is real
the element of danger
"living on the edge"
"walking the thin line"
whatever
however you describe it
it is a part of what I do
and a part of why I do it.

But mostly they ask about the secrets
official or not
who is doing what to whom and why.
And how can they get a piece of it.
Power.

I chose this line of work for the same reason
I imagine
that most of us do: to fight crime
ideal notions of making the world a better place.
But I can't do this anymore
I have discovered a crime that
I am powerless against:
the consequences of my own actions

Yes, people will get hurt
"a necessary sacrifice, but
always for a greater good, right?"
Isn't that right?

I am tired
of holding on to other people's secrets
and living other people's lies
when all I want is to be with her.

I can't think of a "greater good" than this.
I am. In love.

You see? I have a few secrets of my own
here's another one:
Lately I have lost the ability to dream at night
no more Danny Kaye
which is not the main reason why I am resigning
but, for now, it's reason enough.

Scene Sixteen

DOYLE *and* ALISA. *She is fast asleep: the drug has taken effect.*

DOYLE You can come in now.

JOHNNY *enters, carrying a briefcase. He looks at the sleeping figure.*

JOHNNY Is she —

DOYLE She'll be fine. Just a mild sedative. You'll be pleased to know she's agreed to co-operate. Lucky for you.

JOHNNY Yes. Sir.

DOYLE *hands* JOHNNY *a set of keys.*

DOYLE The file is in a tiled safe, under one of the throw rugs. I'll leave it to you to figure out which rug, however.

Beat.

DOYLE You nearly blew it for us. You know that.

JOHNNY Yes, sir.

DOYLE Your instructions were to infiltrate the CLF through the suspect, apprehend File Number 17-C, and begin the standard disinformation procedure: Send the CLF a decoy; something to keep their heads scratching —

JOHNNY Yes, sir. But I —

DOYLE A routine operation. Wouldn't you say? *(beat)* When you came back to us empty-handed, we knew something was up. But I had no idea it was that.

JOHNNY Did she tell you —

DOYLE Yes, but don't worry: I know how sticky these things can be.

JOHNNY *avoids* DOYLE*'s gaze by picking up the last set of photos.*

DOYLE Quite effective, don't you think?

JOHNNY Longest session of my life.

DOYLE Yes, well. You owe a debt of thanks to our make-up artist. I didn't want to have to use them, but she just wouldn't take the bait —

JOHNNY Sir —

DOYLE Yes?

JOHNNY *is silent.*

DOYLE You had her quite convinced, "Johnny." Whatever spell you put on her seemed to work. The way she talked about you? I was almost convinced myself. What did you do? *(beat)* What was it like?

JOHNNY I am resigning, sir.

DOYLE Yes, well. You understand there has to be a full inquiry —

JOHNNY Yes. Sir.

JOHNNY *fingers the photograph.*

DOYLE Keep it. As a souvenir.

JOHNNY No, thank you sir.

DOYLE So. Any plans for your — shall we say — hiatus?

JOHNNY *(looking to the sleeping* ALISA*)* I have a few house calls to make. Who knows? Maybe some dancing lessons.

DOYLE Ah. Dancing. Good. Dancing is good.

They shake hands.

DOYLE Keep in touch?

JOHNNY Oh. You'll always be able to track me down.

Lights fade. Music: Strauss. JOHNNY *dances over to the sleeping* ALISA. *She remains still.* JOHNNY *begins to speak, as the music gets louder, until it finally drowns him out.*

JOHNNY There's this dream I have? Takes place in a motel room. And it's just me. No past, no future, just a constantly changing ever-present. Anyway, in this dream, I am looking for....

Blackout.

The End

Total Body Washout

dedicated to K.K.

You are asked again and again and again
by the men in clean white coats
but even if you could find the words
they would not understand.

Describe the day.
Describe the events.
Describe the feeling.

It lasts only a moment and then it's gone.
But in that moment —

You see the words dangling in front of you
the words are clumsy tools, they are awkward,
they confuse.
They always fall short
of what you really want to say.
But they're all you've got.

Describe the feeling....

Production History

Total Body Washout was originally produced in Toronto at the Alumnae Theatre's New Ideas Festival, 1994. It was performed by Drew Carnwath, and directed and designed by Diana Kolpak. The performance dates were February 5-18, 1994.

Total Body Washout was later produced in Toronto at the Tarragon Theatre, by Whetstone Productions. The performance dates were September 12-22, 1996. It was performed by Robert Tsonos, with the following crew:

Director: Diana Kolpak
Set Design: Wendy Akerboom
Lights Design: Sharon DiGenova
Stage Manager: Steven Moore
Producer: Donna Gall

Characters

JAMES

Scene One

Hospital sounds. Blue light up on JAMES, *who lies sleeping in a stiff hospital bed. He begins to toss and turn. A nightmare. Music.*

Then, a single white light on JAMES' *face. He sits up in his hospital bed. Twitching. Covered in sweat.*

JAMES You are driving. You're a young man, okay?
Twenty-two twenty-four maybe twenty-five.
Thirty-five years old. You're a singer, you sing
I don't know
opera maybe. Yeah opera's good, opera works.
And you're driving.

You're driving, say, from London Ontario where you just performed in Gilbert and Sullivan's 1886 smash hit "Pirates of Penzance," to your apartment in Toronto, downtown Toronto, Cabbagetown.

Nice apartment, big apartment, big like "I just renovated and tore out half my walls" big, not "My God this place so huge I'll never be able to fill it" big.

So so so you're driving driving fast
maybe a hundred maybe a hundred and ten
twenty thirty hell maybe more.

But maybe not maybe just a hundred
but who cares, right?
you're the only one on the road
and it's three in the morning, right?
Highway Four-something.

There you are: Zipping along bombing along
happy zippy bombing along in your 1989 Hyundai.
You turn on the radio and there's some guy
I mean some voice some guy's voice
on the radio
he's talking about the new Right Wing movement
in the United States.

The South will rise again movement.
The Neo-Nazi cross-burning fascist punks
in hooded bedsheets movement.
In The United States of America.
In Decatur Georgia.
In Williamsburg Pennsylvania
and other places too.

And he talks and he talks
and all this talk makes you kind of angry
it reminds you of riots in Los Angeles
it reminds you of your own black friends
it reminds you of something Aunt Ellie once
whispered to you in a crowded room
and the more it reminds you of all these things
the angrier you become until finally you say:

"New Right Wing? New Right Wing?
What about the old Right Wing?
Did they die? Did they go away?
Where did they go?
Greenland for Pete's sake?"

You change the station to find some music
some nice music some mellow music
some good-time easy-listening
calm-you-down-a-bit music
and finally you find a station playing music with a beat
not unlike the beating of your own heart
bah BOOM bah BOOM bah BOOM.

And maybe you're driving a bit too fast
and maybe the fog is beginning to settle over
Highway Four-something from London to Toronto
and maybe you're still thinking about
the New and Improved Right Wing Movement
because that's when it happens —

A big deer in the middle of the road
a big big deer right in the middle of the road —
and of course you hit it.
SMASH!

Something I don't know something goes smash
you pump the brakes
you spin out
you crash into the guardrail
you flip over the guardrail
you land upside down in a ditch
thirty metres away
and you're covered in shattered
something.

You crawl out the back door
because the front door is smashed in
and you're a little shaken up
I mean you're a lot shaken up
and even though it's a good thing a lucky thing
a good and lucky thing that you're even alive
still
you look down and you are covered
totally covered
from head to waist
in blood.

You crawl towards the highway for help
to flag down a car or a truck
or perhaps an emergency vehicle
if you're lucky
but before you even reach the guardrail
you pass out in the ditch.

You lie there unconscious for an hour
before someone
a cop actually
Oh-Pee-Pee
notices an overturned 1989 Hyundai
with expired plates.

And lying there beside the car is its driver
you
covered in fresh red blood.

You'll never know what really happened
the night you narrowly escaped the jaws of death
the night you crawled from the worst accident of your life
the night you took one look at yourself drenched
in the blood of a dead deer...
and fainted.

Scene Two

Hospital sounds. Bright fluorescent lights. Soft pastel colours. Harmless artwork. Room 814 is sparsely furnished with a bed, a table, a bedside lamp, a desk, and a chair with wheels.

JAMES *is sitting in the wheeled chair. He is flipping through a questionnaire. As he reads, he pushes himself back and forth across the room. He is wearing hospital pants, a flannel pyjama top, and fuzzy animal slippers. He speaks into a small tape recorder.*

JAMES "Family name."

Hart. Without an E.

"Given name."

James.

My parents were going to call me Alistair. After Alistair Cooke? Alistair. I like it. Al. I almost changed my name to Alistair. I spent a whole week seriously considering the name Alistair, which I'm sure is longer than most people consider the name Alistair. Even people named Alistair.

But I decided to keep James, because Alistair sounds a bit like "alabaster" and from there who knows where it would go? Imagine being a kid named Alistair. Getting teased in the playground. "Hey Ali-Bastard!" "What's the matter Ali-Baba?" And then —

Beat. JAMES *sighs.*

James William Francis Hart.

"Occupation."

I am a waiter at a downtown restaurant — slash, pick-up joint — known as The Hope and Grope. One of those self-conscious, fake British pubs. That's the aim, anyway. To me the decor is more like Bauhaus meets Walt Disney: functional but Goofy. Currently on leave of absence for professional development.

"Date of birth."

Ten. Oh-nine. Nineteen sixty-nine. September tenth. My birthday. The day I freaked out. The day I —

"Place of birth."

Frogmore, Ontario. I know, I know: inbreeding. Capital of Canada. But that's not why I'm in here. Don't think I didn't do a full geneological check on both parents when I found that out.

I also read somewhere that Frogmore has one of the ten highest crime rates in Canada. Per capita. We moved to Toronto when I was four, when my dad got a new position at head office, but I like to think my parents left Frogmore to protect me from a certain life of crime.

Sure, hindsight's twenty-twenty, but the more I think about it? If we'd stayed in Frogmore, I know I'd have woken up one morning in a cow field next to a headless cheerleader and a bloodstained roulette wheel after a fun-filled night of random violence and sniffing airplane glue. Instead of where I am —

Beat.

Instead of where I am. Room 814. The eighth floor, for mental illness. Psycho sickbay. Bucketville. Patients are called "Buckets." But we are encouraged to use first names. I am a patient.

The official name for what I have — for what happened to me — is an Anxiety Attack.

Into tape recorder:

Aaaagggghh!!! Anxiety Attack!

Apparently the term Nervous Breakdown is no longer acceptable in the medical profession. That's what they say. They also say I need to rest for some, indefinite, period of time. And that it will take a while to "get in touch" with whatever brought this on. I just hope it's not one of those deep dark secrets from my childhood that's been buried in my subconcious for years and years. I mean, that's so cliché.

I asked Dr. Kipling — that's my doctor — "What are the chances of this being the result of a weird and twisted game some authority figure played on me when I was too young to know the difference?"

But he just gave me one of those curious sideways looks — you know the way dogs look at you all crooked? Like you've given them a command they don't understand? Dr. Kipling does that a lot with me. I'm kind of worried about him, actually. He's a nice enough guy, but he tries way too hard to be my friend, and the truth is he's a bit of a dufus. I mean, he still wears Wallabees. And he drives a K-Car. "New Country." But he's the only one in here who will listen to me. Most of the doctors here? It's like they were zipped into a mylar baggie in 1974 and never got out.

Anyway, Dr. Kipling said I have to isolate the areas of my life which give me stress. He said I need to compartmentalize. Swear to God that's how they talk around here. Compartmentalize. Like a huge Tupperware party for all my neuroses. Keep them fresh.

When I first got in here? I had to go through all these interviews and panels and screenings. I'm sure there were twice as many doctors behind the two-way mirror — like in "Goldfinger"? But I didn't make a big stink about it. At the end of every interview they always came back to the same question: "What happened on September tenth?"

"What happened on September tenth?"

Sudden harsh white light up on JAMES. *He stands.*

Well, that was the day I was born, for one,
but that's just a coincidence —
Look, it's no big deal, I'm telling you it was
no different from any other day —
Hey, I didn't ask for your help —
I don't —
I don't want to talk about it, okay?
You wouldn't understand!

Lights resume as before. Beat.

So, I wasn't exactly co-operative with the interview format. They gave me this questionnaire to fill out "at my leisure." Like it's a challenge to fit it into my busy schedule.

And if I don't feel like writing the answers down, I'm allowed to speak them into this tape recorder.

Into tape recorder:

Which is what I'm doing now.

Meanwhile, they've pumped some anti-depressant into me, a happy pill called Prozac. I asked Dr. Kipling: "How will I know when it's begun to work?" He just gave me one of those please-don't-hurt-me-I'm-just-a-bank-teller smiles, and said "you'll know."

They've also got me tranked up on Xanex, because I started to have these intense dreams about roadkills and large antlered animals. Ever notice how drugs have such dippy names? Like newly discovered planets: XANEX.

Anyway, Xanex seems to work. No more dreams. No more... no more anything. What else? I have the attention span of a small chick pea. I'm not good with crowds. I can't get on elevators without freaking out. Which concerns me. I asked the doctors about it, but they had nothing to say. In fact, since that interview? No one has been doing much talking around here. Except me, into the tape recorder. That's ironic. Normally people who talk to themselves this much are called insane. Not me. Nosiree, so long as I keep this tape recorder going — it's called therapy.

Anyway! Crazy talk. Psychobabble. I met some new Buckets today. Always a treat. I have this game I play, where I try to guess the Bucket's illness, like why they're in here. I'll have dinner with a Susan, or watch TV with a Hector, and I'll spend the whole time trying to figure it out.

It's kind of twisted, but it passes the time. Usually they don't give me a chance, they just come right out and say it by way of introduction. Like a conventioner in a hotel lobby:

"Hello, my name is Wanda and I'm on lithium right now!"

"Hi! Steve. I'm suicidal — "

JAMES *trails off. He shivers, and closes his eyes. Then, with real effort:*

I met a cute — I mean cute in a skinny sexy kind of way — I met a cute girl — woman — in art therapy today. Her name is Miranda and she's very talkative and funny and she looks about fourteen years old. But I know she's older than that 'cause you've got to be at least eighteen to be on floor number-eight. Which is a good thing because I'm highly attracted to that pencil-thin-sallow-close-to-death look.

So later on I'm trying to watch TV, 'cause "The Thirty-Nine Steps" is on, one of my all-time favourites, and she sits down right beside me and says: "What a stupid movie."

"Are you kidding? It's a classic."

"Exactly," she says, "It's a classic stupid movie."

So we shoot the breeze for at least an hour, her talking about her family and shit, and me trying to figure out why she's in here — but before I can guess, she asks me:

"So what's wrong with you, anyway?"

"I'm here for a two-week vacation, ha ha. What about you?"

She stares at me, I mean really looks at me for the first time, and says:

"I have an addictive personality."

"Sure you do," I say. "What's your addiction?"

"People," she says, and walks away.

As she walks down the hall, I notice the tiniest tattoo on her ankle. A peace dove.

Beat.

I also notice she's got white cotton bandages wrapped tightly around both wrists.

Light change to surreal effect. Game show music. With an unnatural burst of energy, JAMES *grabs the questionnaire and jumps onto his bed. He speaks in deep radio-announcer voice.*

Good evening, ladies and gentlemen, I'm Big Jimbo Jackson, your host for tonight's exciting episode of "What's My Damage?"

"What's My Damage?" — the show where you, the contestant, try to identify the mental illness of our celebrity guest in less than twenty questions!

Sound of crowd cheering.

Here are the clues. And remember, no help from the studio audience!

One: Do you hear voices?
If so, what do they say?

Two: Do you believe in life after death
or is it the other way around?

Three: Circle the following qualities
which you feel best describe yourself:

Increasing sound of applause.

Are you easy-going? athletic? generous? moody? stubborn? demanding? conceited? lecherous? pathetic? worthless? loud? ugly? stupid? sadistic? satanic? psychotic?

Sound of loud buzzer to deafening applause.

JAMES *collapses, bends over, and holds his stomach. Lights slowly fade to black.*

I —
Sorry, Big Jimbo, I —
don't feel feel like playing.

Scene Three

JAMES *is sitting on his bed. He is flipping through a large dictionary.*

JAMES There must be a German word for what's wrong with me.

Gotta love the Germans. They have these humongous words to describe what no one else can; these states of angst and desire.

Here's one. "Weltanshuang" — meaning world view. Nope. "Wanderlust" — desire to travel. Nice, but no. "Schadenfreude" — the pleasure we take in other people's misfortune —

Beat. JAMES *sighs, and puts down the dictionary.*

Dr. Kipling paid me an unscheduled visit today. I said "What's up, Doc?" and he said he's been listening to my tapes. He said I have a vivid imagination, but that my grasp of the purpose of the tapes was tenuous. At first I thought he meant, like, ten times better than he expected. But then I looked up the word "tenuous."

Anyway, he also said I was making progress — which to me suggests a movement from point-A to point-B, right? A progression from somewhere to somewhere else? Right?

But so far I haven't gone anywhere. I'm still here. Floor number eight. It's kind of creepy up here on floor number eight. All these soft pastel colours and plastic user-friendly smiles. It's timeless up here, too: I never know what time of day it is. A couple of times I forgot what city I was in. Hospitals do that to you. They slowly shut out the rest of the world. Television and visiting hours —

Beat.

God I could use a cigarette! We're only allowed to smoke in the lounge, the TV room, and half of the cafeteria. But not in our rooms. Which is just as well, 'cause lately I've bummed too many butts off the Buckets.

Where was I? O yeah, the creepiest thing about floor number eight is that the main elevator system by-passes the floor completely. It glides mysteriously from seven to nine, like some bad horror movie from the seventies: "Floor Number Eight," starring Karen Black, Oliver Reed, and Rod Steiger as the journalist who finally reveals the sticky and sordid truth about: FLOOR NUMBER EIGHT!

To get here you've got to take the MacKenzie Wing elevators. Which is only three miles from here. Not that I care —

This morning I tried to get on the elevator. Just to see. Just to see if I could do it. I was doing fine until some doctors I didn't recognize got on, all these doctors, and they pressed buttons to floors I'd never been to, I mean buttons to floors I didn't want to go to, my throat seized up my heart grew two sizes too big just like the Grinch until I thought it was going to burst through my chest I started to make these wheezing sounds and I heard this voice in the back of my head I heard this voice cry out:

"Someone get a doctor!"

Which at the time was kind of funny, but right now I don't think it's funny. It's not very funny at all.

Beat.

That's why I got an unscheduled visit today. He said I should rest. What? And miss art therapy? I would rather chew on tin foil!

I love finger painting: getting all messy and abstract like Jackson Pollock. Jack the Dripper. Sheila the art therapist, this mousey tweed-jacket of a woman, says the point of the exersize is to paint how we feel.

"What a coincidence! We're out of black paint again!"

Next week we get to keep our paintings —

"What, aren't you going to send them down to the lab for analysis?"

"No," she says, "This is about process, not product."

They really do talk this way around here.

Right before the Good Doctor left this morning he gave me some relaxation tapes. To be played, I imagine, when I'm not tenuously shooting my mouth off to no one in particular.

JAMES *picks up several cassette tapes.*

Let's see. "Solitudes, Part Five: The Loons of Lake Temagemi." Hmmm....

He smashes the tape with the dictionary, and makes loon sounds. He picks another tape.

"Gregorian Chants of the 12th Century, sung by The Brothers of St. Francis." All — right!

JAMES *puts the tape in the player and presses "play." Indeed, we hear Gregorian chants.* JAMES *sings along for a bit.*

So it's just me today. Hangin' with the Brothers in my special room. Why special? Well! I made a discovery. When I woke up this morning — that is, before the fun on the elevator — my tongue felt kinda funny. Like corduoroy or something.

I got up and spent half an hour scrutinizing my mouth in the mirror. Sure enough, there were all these striations along my tongue. Not corduoroy, though. More like volcanic rock formations.

I looked closer and I realized — those marks aren't on my tongue at all. It was it was the plastic coating on the mirror. Plastic coating. Wait a minute.

I started to look around the room for something, anything, with which one could inflict some kind of wound. Nothing. No corners, no sharp edges, no racks or hooks for hanging bedsheet nooses: Someone sat down and designed this room, a room in which no harm can ever come to its occupant.

Psycho-safe. Freak-free. Bucket-proof. A room where everything — from the mirror to the colour scheme — is completely harmless. Even the art. Now there's a concept: Harmless Art. As opposed to what?

Gregorian chants get louder.

Blackout.

Scene Four

Schoolyard sounds. Children's voices, nursery rhymes. A single white light — the same as in Scene Two — reveals JAMES *in bed.*

JAMES You are nine years old.

You are sitting in your grade five classroom beside your best friend and class clown Sandy Fraser. Sandy has bright red hair that stands straight up and hundreds of freckles all over his face. You get in trouble for trying to connect all of Sandy's freckles with a felt-tipped pen, dot-to-dot.

Your teacher, Mr. Sobaniac, sends both of you down to the office; but getting in trouble isn't such a bad thing so long as Sandy is with you.

After school the fun begins. You and Sandy shoplift family-sized bags of M&Ms. You flash *Playboy* centrefolds in front of old people. You steal hood ornaments from expensive cars. You are the trouble boys.

Sandy loves to get attention. He turns his eyelids inside out. He scotch-tapes dead flies to the school-bus window. He taunts and teases little Alida Krakauer until she's in tears. He throws violent temper tantrums when he doesn't get his way. His parents give him a special pill to calm him down... but it doesn't work.

When Mr. Sobaniac tries to keep Sandy after school for calling him "Sobaniac the Maniac," Sandy runs to the chalkboard and kicks a container of rulers clear across the room. When Mr. Sobaniac threatens to expel him, Sandy stabs Mr. Sobaniac in the leg with a compass.

After that they move Sandy into another classroom. And then to another school. You don't know how to feel. They say he's a bad influence and a dangerous friend, but you miss him because he was never mean to you. He was never mean to you. You never see him again.

Until this night.

On this night you are alone at home.
The doorbell rings
and you open the door to see
Sandy Fraser.
He's a grown man now
he's wearing a tuxedo that's way too small
he's carrying a bouquet of flowers
and even though he's a grown man
he's still got that wild look in his eyes
as if he might eat you
or burst into tears.

And even though it wasn't your fault
you want to say I'm sorry
you want to say I tried to give you a chance
but somehow the words come out all wrong
and Sandy just smiles
and hands you the flowers
and as he walks away you hear him sing:

"I am rubber, you are glue.
It bounces off me and sticks to you."

Scene Five

The sound of hammering. JAMES *is covering the still-life hospital print with his own finger-painting, which is firey-red and chaotic. He is wearing a doctor's white lab-coat.*

JAMES Ta-da! Harmful art!

JAMES *looks at the tape recorder, sighs, and then presses the record button.*

I know I know, it's been a while. Truth is I've been spending a lot of time with Miranda. She's very entertaining in a near-death kind of way. Yesterday we went on a tear around the hospital, just for the hell of it, just to break the spell of boredom that can suck us Buckets dry if we're not careful.

Waiting for the elevator was like waiting for the electric chair. But when I got on with Miranda? I held my breath and — nothing happened. I was fine. Miranda kept looking at me like I was a space alien, but I didn't care: I, James Hart, can now ride the elevators!

We went down to the laundry room and stole these doctor scrubs. This lab coat is like a skeleton key: You can go anywhere you want and no one questions your authority. Heck, no one even notices you —

Beat. JAMES *shivers.*

You can learn quite a lot in hospitals. Here's one: TBW — Total Body Washout. That's a special room where they, the doctors, hook you up to this machine that slowly sucks the blood out of you, cleans it, then slowly pumps it back in. Isn't that great?

It's still you, but "New and Improved." Would you feel any different afterwards? There's something warm and dark about it. The sound of it. Total. Body. Washout.

Then we went down to the Waste Disposal Floor. You would not believe the things you can find in hospital garbages — if you can handle the smell. It's a goldmine down there! Like a huge, surreal garage sale. I fished out some old X-rays and gave them to Miranda. And the way she reacted? You'd think she'd won the lottery or something. She held it up to the light and said:

"That's the thing about X-rays. They're never just black-and-white, but all the shades of grey in between — like life itself."

She always says weird shit like that.

"If we break enough watches, we can make time stand still."

Miranda's definitely out there — not too tightly wrapped — but in a very sane and honest way. I mean we can sit in silence for hours, playing cards or watching the soaps or whatever, and out of the blue she'll say:

"Clouds exist so we don't take the sun for granted."

And I know how hokey it sounds. But coming from her mouth, it — it makes a whole lot of sense.

I found out why — I mean the real reason — why she's in here. About a year ago she woke up one day and decided she wasn't going to eat for a while. When that little while turned into a few months, her parents got concerned. They called it anorexia, she called it a hunger strike. I call it just plain stupid, but of course I'd never say that. In front of her. So I asked her about it.

"Hunger strike, huh? What are you protesting?"

"Food," she said.

"Look, how can you live without food? It's the greatest thing on earth. It's even better than sex."

She stared at me and said:

"As far as experience goes, great food still doesn't compare with even bad sex."

"Yes it does — I should know!"

Beat.

How did I get on to this? Oh yeah — part of the reason we're hanging out these days is that she actually has an appetite with me. Like, all her hang-ups and fears about food disappear when we eat together, alone in her room. Which I suppose is a compliment. So I'm making an effort to be around for meals, which I don't mind, 'cause the last time I ate in the cafeteria one of the other Buckets stole my Evian bottle, blessed it as holy water, and poured it over my head, calling me the "Anti-James."

Since Miranda told me her story she keeps asking me: "Why are you in here? You seem normal enough to me. What's wrong with you, anyway?" As if I know. As if I could just —

Beat. JAMES *hops off his bed, and pulls the questionnaire out from a pile of clothes.*

Me? I'm here for the fun questionnaires — it's worth the drive to Bucketville. Let's see. Question Twelve:

"List and describe, in brief, any history of mental illness in your family."

Do they mean, like, diagnosed? In spite of having me for a son, I've never worried about my parents. They're too sensible: To them, insanity is just a waste of valuable time.

I do have a crazy aunt — I know, who doesn't, right? — but this is more than just funny stories at family picnics.

Elizabeth. Aunt Ellie. We saw her quite a bit when we were kids — every Christmas and most summers. I can't remember the last time I saw her, because —

This one Christmas? Ellie painted all the house plants sparkly red and green, and some of them were gold and silver. I thought it was neat — and kind of weird — but very festive nonetheless, and later I asked my Mom why she never did cool stuff like that.

I remember the expression on Uncle Pete's face as he tried to make a joke out of it, how —

"One of these days I should let Ellie out of the house to get a real job."

But nobody laughed.

After dinner my cousin Jodie said that when her mom ran out of green and red paint she started in on the nail polish.

"At least fifty bucks worth," Jodie said.

That was the first time I realized Aunt Eilie wasn't like most people.

Once, when we were invited over for dinner, Uncle Pete came home after work that day to find nothing prepared — Ellie hadn't cooked anything. She'd tried to make a spaghetti sauce, but when she filled the pressure cooker with tomatoes it exploded and sent the tomatoes flying all over the kitchen.

So! She went out and bought ten tubs of Baskin Robbins Ice Cream, because it was Uncle Pete's favourite and she wanted to surprise him. Well. He was surprised. But he never got mad at her. This time he just threw the ice cream out and called Fenton's for catering.

And that was the scene in the kitchen when we arrived: Aunt Ellie scraping the hardened tomato off the floor with a letter opener. Uncle Pete tossing whole tubs of Chunky Monkee Ice Cream into the backyard. And my cousin Jodie standing in between them, crying.

JAMES *absently begins to flick his lighter on and off.*

Ellie lives at Ongwanada now. That's a special hospital outside Kingston where families deposit their resident whackos when they become too much trouble. Or too embarassing. There was never any room for madness in my family. My grandfather was determined on that point. My grandmother, too: appearance is everything. If you're going to go bonkers, just do it quietly, dear, and don't tell the Joneses. Everything will be fine. Pass the watercress, would you darling? Everything will be fine —

Fucking hypocrites. It's not that easy. My Aunt Ellie had it right. I think she was as sharp as a pin; she was just having fun, fer chrissakes! You want crazy? I'll tell you what crazy is — crazy is living in that house, living that life — no job, no fun, bored beyond recognition. Talking to those painted plants 'cause they're the only things left for you to love anymore.

Nothing left to do but wait... and wait and wait for the day when the waiting can end.

JAMES *flicks the lighter faster and faster.*

There once was a boy from Berlin.
People laughed at his crazy grin.
But he didn't care 'cause they weren't aware
that he lived in the looney bin....

Root-a-toot-toot, root-a-toot-toot.
I just got out of the institute....

As the lights dim, JAMES *holds his hand over the flame and moves it closer. And closer. A test.*

Scene Six

Night. The sound of JAMES *singing. Off-key. Lights up to an empty hospital room.* JAMES *tears into the room, singing at full volume. He tosses a brown paper parcel on to the bed, and begins to dance.*

JAMES Ba-bum ba-ba ba-ba bum-ba — Prozac!

Okay, yes, the drugs finally kicked in, but that's not the reason for my sunny disposition. Nosiree. Today — tonight — I have a date with Miranda!

Well okay not a date exactly, but since I am now completely elevator-friendly we're going on another tour! This time it's up to the maternity ward to check out the new humans.

Gotta love babies. They're just like your favorite adults, only smaller, and they don't say stupid things.

He sings:

There's something due anyday
I will know right away —
soon as it shows....

Dr. Kipling poked his face in here for a nanosecond today, just long enough to remind me why I will never be like him. The poor man doesn't know how to maintain eye contact! So when he said, vaguely, that "things" were improving, I thought he was talking about his own problems, not mine....

But wait, there's more! I got a care package from the guys down at The Hope and Grope. Let's see:

"Dear James. Hope you're doing well. Try not to get too crazy. Can you work for me Friday night, ha ha."

He opens the package.

Cigarettes! Wine gums... *Sunday New York Times...* emergency candles... clean underwear.... Yes! They remembered!

JAMES *pulls out a cassette tape and places it in the player: "The Girl From Ipanema." He snaps his fingers and engages in pre-date rituals.*

You gotta cut me some slack here. This is the first time I've felt anything even approaching sexual desire since Christmas seventy-nine. The moment I got in here, I knew my sex drive was completely shot. I even tried monsterbating for the first time since I was nineteen. But I'm still not very good at it.

Monsterbating. I was never very good at it. Even as a kid. It wasn't doing for me what it was supposed to — at least it wasn't doing for me what it was doing for everyone else. Either that or I was just doing it wrong — what are you going to do, ask someone to supervise?

Hey Billy, what are you doing after school? Do you wanna come over to my place? I don't think I've got a handle on this thing....

But with Miranda, it's a happy surprise because — well, I've been single for a long time. A kind of self-imposed celibacy for all those sensible, self-discovery bullshit reasons. You know. The kind of advice your friends give you all the time. When you don't ask for it:

"You need to be on your own for a while."

"You need to learn how to love yourself before you can love someone else."

"You need to discover the difference between real loneliness and just being alone."

Beat. JAMES *turns the music off.*

You need a shot to the head.

My last relationship? Valerie. Like the Monkees song. She was the Assistant Equipment Manager for the Montreal Canadiens. We were introduced one night between periods, and the way she was handling the water bottles? My heart went ping. Love on ice.

We had a great time together, no matter what we did. Playing euchre 'til three in the morning. Getting high on jasmine tea. All those sugary, morning-after sex kisses over the Saturday Cryptic Crossword —

It wasn't built to last. It's my loss. I know that. She's one of the smartest people I've met — I haven't had a single good idea since she left. I haven't spoken to her, either. I want to, and I've thought about it, but —

Right after we broke up, her father died. But I never knew about it. No one told me. Three months later her cat Attilla dies, and this I hear about. Word got to me that Attilla had died at a New Year's Eve party when she tried to eat an entire ham. Oh, God. And it just killed her: Too much ham.

So I sent her a note of condolence over the death of Attilla the cat, entirely ignorant of her father's death. I remember writing:

"Now I take this pen in hand and reflect upon the loss of those closest to us."

She must have thought: "What about my father, you cretin? You didn't even like Attila!"

I think she needs some time to, you know, heal.

We broke up almost a year ago, when I —
I just wish I could —
Go back, and —

It started out with one innocent little lie —
and hell, everybody does it —
I said I was one place
when in fact I was somewhere else.

Or I said I felt one thing
when in fact I felt... something else.

I thought I was protecting her from the truth
it felt like it was the best thing
the only thing I could do, but —

Soon I —
I had to tell a whole spiderweb of other lies
these huge, damaging lies just to support
that first one.

Five full beats.

Miranda's waiting.

Scene Seven

JAMES *is standing. Bright interrogation lights.*

JAMES You are asked again and again and again
by the men in clean white coats
but even if you could find the words
they would not understand.

Describe the day.
Describe the events.
Describe the feeling.
It's just a moment, and then it's gone.
But in that moment —

I see the words dangling in front of me.
The words are clumsy tools. They confuse.
They are awkward.
They always fall short
of what I really want to say.
But they're all we've got.

Describe the feeling.

Once upon a time
you are a small person
swinging on a playground swing.
You pump and pull and pump and pull
higher and higher
until you reach that point
where you are going neither up nor down
forwards or backwards.

It lasts only a second
you are suspended in time and space.
The rush in your stomach —
the laws of gravity are turned upside down —
is like nothing you've ever experienced.

Or later still at the top of a roller coaster.
After the slow climb up
and before the wild ride down
there is a tugging at your chest
as you reach the top
just for a moment.

And it too is a rush
because from where you are
you can see everything
the pink and blue cotton candy
the little lost children
the tour buses in the parking lot
the faces of other people on the ferris wheel
across the park.

In that moment you feel utterly alone
but for the first time in your life you like that feeling
you want to remember it
protect it

you desperately want to know
how to recapture the wonderful loneliness
at the top of the roller coaster
where everything seems so clear to you
you wonder if there's a name for it
you wonder why these things only happen
in playgrounds
and amusement parks
and you look for some significance in that
but of course there isn't.

Because the moment has passed
and you wonder
finally
if you will ever know that feeling again
and it saddens you to think you won't
and no one will understand or believe you
no one will feel the way you felt
ever again
not even you.

Scene Eight

Later the same evening. JAMES *enters his room slowly and sits on the corner of his bed. He lights a cigarette.*

JAMES Fucking bastards.

Beat. JAMES *shivers.*

So I go to pick up Miranda for our visit to the newly-humans.

But when I knock on her door she —
She isn't there.
She was —

She'd refused to eat her lunch because she said she honestly wasn't feeling well. They kept her in that room, that fucking smelly room with the piss-yellow walls and the puke-green floors and the banging radiators, until she ate every last bite. Three hours they kept her in there. And when she finally managed to force down all the cold fish and boiled vegetables, they said:

"No. All of it."

A piece of pie. A fucking piece of frozen lemon pie, and they wouldn't let her out until she finished it. That's when she snapped.

According to Kayla the candy-striper, Miranda started screaming and throwing things. Including the pie. Which landed behind the radiator. And an ashtray. Which went through the TV screen: "Top Cops."

They've got her strapped down and whacked out on... something. When I got there, she didn't even recognize me. She couldn't even talk. I wanted to wait there beside her until she came to, but the intern told me visiting hours were over.

So I told him he was a goat-blowing hermaphrodite. That's when Miranda woke up. She said:

"That probably wasn't the smartest thing to do."

"You're one to talk! It probably wasn't a smart thing to chuck an ashtray through the TV."

But she said she'd seen that episode already.

"Why didn't you just eat the fucking pie and have done with it?"

She shook her head and said:

"It's not the food. It's about control. I'm a control freak."

"With an addictive personality. There's a combo plate for you. If you can't stand the heat, stay out of the kitchen."

Then she leaned over and whispered:

"It's not the heat. It's the humility. I thought I was in control of this thing. But it's controlling me. You wouldn't understand. And why should I tell you anything? You won't even tell me why you're in here!"

Miranda had no idea.

Light change.

Okay, fine.
You want to know why I'm here?
I'll tell you.
I'm in here because I chose to be.
Alright?
I admitted myself.

Beat.

I had just returned from a long trip to the west coast. The Jack Kerouac thing. Hell, everybody does it.

So I figured I should go out there and see for myself what all the fuss was about. But I didn't know what I was looking for, so big surprise when I didn't find it. I didn't even find myself, like that joke about California, remember that joke?

"Wherever you go — there you are."

It's true. I bought a bunch of postcards. But I didn't mail them. Every place I went, another postcard shoved into my knapsack. Soon I got homesick for the smallest, silliest things. Daily mail. My coffee mug. My music.

But when I got home I just —
I lay in bed for three days.
I didn't call anyone.
I just lay there thinking.

About what I can't remember.
I just lay there eating nothing but saltine crackers
and orange-juice
hermetically sealed
checking the phone for a dial tone
seven times a day.

I wasn't expecting anyone to call.
Nobody knew I was home.

Then the phone did ring
it was Murray the manager
from The Hope and Grope
asking me to pick up a shift the next day
September tenth
my birthday.

I didn't mind going in on my birthday
honestly
I was happy
I had an excuse to get out of bed.

So I go into the restaurant
and I'm real glad to see the guys
and real glad to help out Murray
and real glad to be useful
at something
but
I guess it's too much too soon
and something —

Something twigs
I don't know
I forget to ask for drinks
I start to sweat like crazy
I mess up the orders
and right in the middle of serving this woman
who looks a bit like Mia Farrow
I know I have to get out of the restaurant
so I do
I —

I run out of the restaurant
and get into my car
without even closing my tables
I just run out
and drive
past the dollar store
past the liquor store
faster and faster
I have to get the hell out.

I make it as far as Rosedale Valley Road
this deep ravine
cutting right into the heart of the city
I get as far as the flower seller
and I see that he's waving up
way up
to one of the bridges
so I look up
way up
and I see this guy standing on the bridge
this guy with bright red hair
standing straight up
in the middle of the bridge
and he's looking down at the drivers
at me
with a wild look in his eyes and I —
I have to look away
back to the road.

When I pass under the bridge
I look in my mirror to see him
but all I see is his body hit the ground
behind me
and it bounced
he bounced.

I stop the car and run over to him
his legs are splayed apart
his arms are tucked under his body
he looks like some child's marionette that's
been dropped and abandoned for another toy.

Somebody calls the police
and I watch
a crowd of people stand around his body
shaking their heads
like a herd of stupid animals.

When the police arrive
they ask a few questions
and I am free to go
only
I can't go
I can't leave yet
I just have to take a closer look
at his face
just to see.

Beat.

But I didn't.
What difference would it've made.
I saw him
whoever he was
he looked at me
the last person he saw alive
and we were the same person
I knew.

Oh God he drew me in with his gaze
like a secret
and I looked away.

It was a movie I'd already seen before
in my head
I knew how it ended.

So when he landed on the roadway
like that
I wasn't shocked or surprised
I was just
numb.

Beat.

I don't remember too much of what happened
after that
except that I fell on to my knees
and dug my nails into the pavement
and I started to howl like a stupid animal myself.

I wanted to start over
start everything over
go to a place where no one knew me
recreate a me I could live with
free from all the lies
that's why I went out west in the first place
right
but I blew it
right
so I came here instead.

We spend our whole lives looking for
something
and just when we think we're getting close
we realize we don't know what it is.

Some people give up
some people keep looking
harder and harder
but it doesn't get them anywhere
except Rosedale Valley Road.

Some people end up here
only to be pushed and prodded
by white lab coats.

"Come on champ
you can do it
get back out there
here take these pills
they'll make you feeeeeeel better
don't worry
the world will be a better place
when you get healthy."

Well, what if it's not?

What if nothing I do will make any difference?

What if I wake up one day to discover that
what I thought was my passion
is now simply how I pass the time?

Just waiting
that's why Aunt Ellie went crazy
it was finally the only way to deal with
a life that had nothing more to offer.

As soon as my cousin Jodie was old enough
to take care of herself
there was nothing left
for Ellie to do but wait.

And if that's it
if all I have to look forward to is
waiting to die
well
there are plenty of perfectly good bridges
kaboom
from zero to God in twenty seconds.

I'm not afraid of dying.
Miranda taught me that.
It's the rest of my life that terrifies me.

Slow to black. Drumming.

Scene Nine

Warm light on JAMES, *no longer in the hospital room. His trousers are rolled up. He holds a postcard, and reads from it.*

JAMES Dear Miranda.
Howdy howdy from the middle of nowhere.
Also known as the Valley.
They say it never rains here.
Yesterday it rained.
Today it rained.
I don't mind it, though.
I'm learning to dodge the raindrops.
And it puts me to sleep.

Things are okay, I guess
but don't worry
I'm still screwed up.
What can I say?
I decided to give myself another chance
out here
because wherever you go —

And speaking of screwed up.
Welcome to the world of out-patient-hood.
Another day another drug.

I miss you.
Do you think soon you'll be able to join me here?
I can't promise you'll find yourself, but
there is one helluva roller-coaster next door.
I'll save you a seat.

Running out of space
stop
say hey to Kipling
stop
it's not the heat its the humanity
stop
whatever you do don't stop to think
or think to stop
stop
gotta go now or soon I won't be able to....

Blackout.

The End.